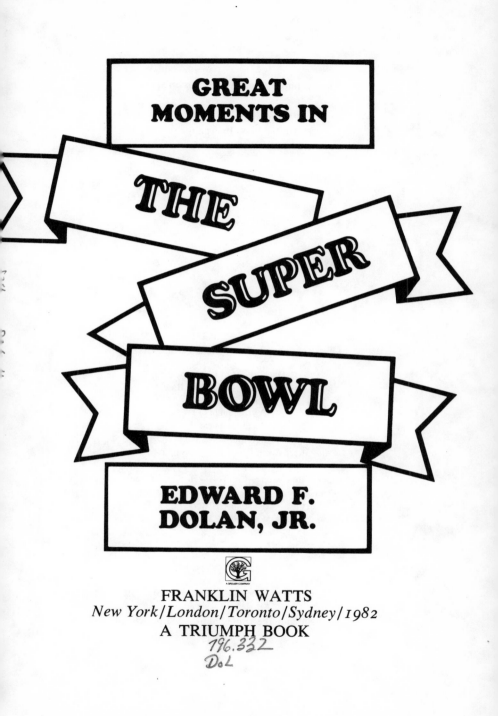

GREAT MOMENTS IN

THE

SUPER

BOWL

EDWARD F. DOLAN, JR.

FRANKLIN WATTS
New York/London/Toronto/Sydney/1982
A TRIUMPH BOOK

Cover photo courtesy of Focus on Sports

Photographs all courtesy of
United Press International

Library of Congress Cataloging in Publication Data

Dolan, Edward F., 1924–
Great moments in the Super Bowl.

(A Triumph book)
Includes index.
Summary: Describes the teams and events of the
first fifteen Super Bowl championship football
games.
1. Super Bowl Game (Football)—History—Juvenile
literature.   [1. Super Bowl Game (Football)—
History.   2. Football—History]   I. Title.
GV956.2.S8D64   796.332'64'09   82-2034
ISBN 0-531-04408-4   AACR2

R.L. 3.0 Spache Revised Formula

CONTENTS

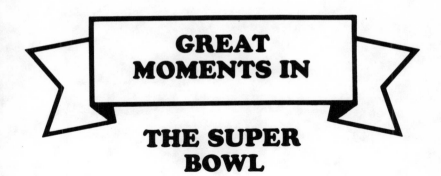

GREAT MOMENTS IN
THE SUPER BOWL

CHAPTER 1

THE GREAT FIRST HALF

The ball sailed high and deep on the opening kick-off. It came down on the Green Bay Packers' 5 yard line. Herb Adderley made the catch. He headed upfield behind his blockers. The Kansas City Chiefs nailed him hard at his 25.

It was January 15, 1967. One of the most historic games in professional sports was under way — Super Bowl I. Two teams were ready to battle for the country's football championship. They were the Packers of the National Football League (NFL) and the Chiefs of the American Football League (AFL).

The two leagues had never played against each other before. But they were bitter rivals. The NFL was the older of the two. It had been around since 1920. Thanks to the NFL, pro football had become a major American sport. The AFL had been started in 1960 by a group of wealthy businessmen.

At first, the NFL had looked down its nose at the AFL. Surely the newcomer wouldn't last. But the infant league *did* last. It grew in popularity. Its owners paid top salaries for good players. They lured some stars away from the NFL. They also acquired a string of top college prospects.

The two leagues soon found themselves in a "money war." Each tried to outbid the other for players. By 1966, things had gotten out of hand. Both leagues felt they were in danger of going broke.

They decided that there was one way to save themselves. They must merge into a single league. The new outfit would be called the National Football League. It would be divided into two conferences. The National Football Conference would be formed from the old NFL teams. The American Football Conference would be formed from the AFL teams. At the end of each season, the champions of the two conferences would play each other for the national title. That battle would be called the "AFL-NFL World Championship Game."

That name was a tongue twister! So the leagues and the press soon found a nickname: the Super Bowl. The nickname stuck. It finally became the game's official title.

The two leagues knew they couldn't complete the details of the merger until 1970. But they decided to stage Super Bowl I right away, at the end of the 1966 season. Each league would play its regular schedule for the season. Each would come up with a champion of its own. Then the two champions would meet on the second Sunday in January, 1967.

And so here were the Packers and the Chiefs facing each other in the Los Angeles Memorial Coliseum. There were 61,946 fans in the stands. The two teams lined up for the first plays from scrimmage. They were about to make football history.

Packer quarterback Bart Starr tried a series of passes and runs. The Chiefs fought back with vicious blitzes. Twice, they sacked Starr. Packer flankerback Boyd Dowler was injured on a hard hit. He had to leave the field. Veteran end Max McGee replaced him. Green Bay was forced to punt.

The Coliseum crowd and the 60 million people watching on TV were surprised. They had expected Green Bay to roll over Kansas City from the start. After all, the Packers had won four NFL crowns since 1960. They had taken the last crown by beating the tough Dallas Cowboys. That championship game had brought them to this first Super Bowl.

Further, the Pack was a veteran unit with plenty of football savvy. It had a hard-hitting offense and a murderous defense. And the team was coached by Vince Lombardi. He was known as the best of the best. A Super Bowl win would be a cinch.

But the Chiefs had stopped the Pack cold on the first series of downs. Everyone knew Coach Hank Stram's men were good. They had hammered the Buffalo Bills 31–7 in the AFL championship game. But everyone believed they were too young to be a match for the experienced Packers. In fact, most fans felt that *no* team in the infant AFL could handle the rugged NFL outfits.

Well, maybe everyone was wrong. Maybe an AFL team could put up a real fight after all.

It certainly looked that way in the next minutes. As soon as KC got the ball, quarterback Len Dawson tested the Packer defense with a run. It went nowhere. But then a cheer burst from the stands. Len dropped back to pass. He connected with left end Chris Burford. The Chiefs had a first down on

Green Bay's 48. But the drive went no farther. The Chiefs punted.

Now the Packers began to move. The Chiefs tried their blitzes again. This time, they didn't work. Bart Starr showed the form that had made him a legend. He fired a shot to right end Marv Fleming. Then there were bullets to halfback Elijah Pitts and left end Carroll Dale. Suddenly, the ball was on KC's 37. The stage was set for the first big play in Super Bowl history.

Max McGee was still substituting for the injured Boyd Dowler. The 205-pound (92-kg) end charged to the 19 as Starr moved back into the pocket. Max made his turn. The ball came sailing in his direction. He saw KC defensive back Willie Mitchell closing in fast for an attempted interception.

Bart sent the pass high to avoid the interception. The ball struck McGee's outstretched hands and bounced away. It sailed overhead and started to come down behind him. Max shot his hand to the rear. He threw himself at the ball. It smacked into his hand. He held on. Then he whirled away from the hard-charging Willie Mitchell. He headed for the goal line.

Nineteen yards later, he was in the end zone. He'd made the Super Bowl's first touchdown!

McGee's one-handed grab was a spectacular

sight. Max was a fine player. But he was at the end of his career after 12 years in the NFL. In fact, he'd planned to retire at the end of the game. He had been used only as a substitute recently. And he'd caught just three passes during the regular season. Today, he would haul in seven. And he would change his mind about retiring.

Don Chandler kicked the point after touchdown (PAT). The PAT was good. The score stood 7–0.

Many of the fans were disappointed. After the first series of plays, they'd hoped for a good fight by KC. Now they wondered if the Chiefs had folded.

They hadn't. Right after the kickoff, the Chiefs took to the air. Dawson delighted the crowd with fakes and play action. And he completely stumped the Packer defense. He arrived at Green Bay's 7 early in the second period. Len backpedaled to the 17 on the next play. He pumped, faked a throw to

Green Bay's Max McGee
makes one of his seven
receptions in Super Bowl I.
This pass was good for
13 yards and a TD.

one receiver, and released the ball. It sailed to Curtis McClinton near the goal line. The big fullback pulled it in and ran into the end zone. A successful PAT by Mike Mercer tied the score at 7–7.

The Coliseum rocked with thunder. The Chiefs hadn't folded after all! They were still putting up a fight — a top-notch fight.

But so was Green Bay. The Pack now ran a smart mix of rushing and passing plays. They fought off hard KC blitzes. Slowly but surely, they moved the ball to the Chiefs' 14. Then Bart Starr handed off to running back Jim Taylor. Taylor swept wide. Blockers Jerry Kramer and Fuzzy Thurston opened a path for him. He himself plowed through several tacklers. He dove across the goal line. Another PAT made the score 14–7.

Now it was KC's turn to look good. There were more fakes, more play action, and more Dawson passes. Soon the Chiefs were on the Green Bay 24. The attack stalled there. There were just 58 seconds left in the period. Mike Mercer trotted in for a field goal attempt. He drove the ball neatly between the uprights.

The half ended with the score at 14–10.

The Coliseum buzzed all during the intermission. Everyone said that it had been a great first half. The Chiefs had kept Green Bay from rolling over them. An AFL team *could* take the best that the NFL had to offer. They were just 4 points behind. Could they do as well in the next half?

The answer came early in the third quarter. KC was in its own territory. Dawson backed into the pocket. The Packers usually didn't do much pass rushing. But now they threw a hard blitz at Len. Tacklers closed in on him fast. He could fold up and take the loss. But instead, the quarterback tried a desperation throw. The pass was a wobbly one. It dropped into the arms of Packer safetyman Willie Woods on his own 45.

Willie took off for the goal line. Every Chief on the field gave chase. They finally caught him 5 yards from pay dirt.

But they might as well have let him go the rest of the way. Starr handed off to Elijah Pitts on the next play. The running back streaked into the end zone. The PAT put Vince Lombardi's team ahead 21–10.

With that touchdown, the Pack took control of the game. KC fought back, but it was no use. The experience of the veterans was paying off. Again, they brought the ball to within the shadow of the Chiefs' goalposts. Then Bart Starr picked Max McGee as his target. He fired a 13-yard bullet. It sent Max into the end zone for his second tally of the day. The PAT gave Green Bay a commanding 28–10 lead.

The fourth quarter saw yet another Packer touchdown (TD). Elijah Pitts took the handoff on KC's 1-yard line and slammed home. With the PAT, the score was 35–10. It stayed there until the final gun turned Super Bowl I into history.

The Packers had taken the first Super Bowl win. The Chiefs walked quietly off the field. Yes, the men from Kansas City had taken a beating. But they could be proud. They had played a fine season. And that day they had put in a great first half. They were second only to the champions of the whole country.

Super Bowl I caused an argument among football fans everywhere. Some said it proved the young AFL couldn't handle an NFL team. Others claimed that the first half had shown that the Chiefs *were* a match for the NFL. They just hadn't been strong enough to stand up to the Packers for a full 60 minutes. Hardly any team in either league was *that* strong.

But the fans all agreed on one point. Both teams had given Super Bowl I some moments of thrilling football action. They were sure every future Super Bowl would do the same. How right they were!

CHAPTER 2

JOE NAMATH KEEPS A PROMISE

The next great moments came in Super Bowl II. The AFL and NFL champions for 1967 were pitted against each other. The game was played on Sunday, January 14, 1968, at Miami's Orange Bowl.

SUPER BOWL II
GREEN BAY PACKERS (NFL)
vs.
OAKLAND RAIDERS (AFL)

Three passes were the highlights of Super Bowl II.

The first pass came in the second quarter. Bart Starr took the snap on his own 38. Eyes narrow, he checked his receivers. He sighted Boyd Dowler breaking into the clear. The Raiders had failed to cover the big left end. Starr didn't hesitate an instant. He fired the ball to Dowler. Then he watched Boyd take off for the goal line. It was a 62-yard touchdown play.

Starr had to wait until the third period for his next big toss. This time, he sent a short pass to Max McGee. Max hadn't retired after Super Bowl I. He had decided to stick around for another season. Now he caught the ball at his own 42. He turned and battled his way for 33 yards. Then the Raiders wrestled him to the ground at their 25.

Max retired at game's end. The reception was his final important play for the Pack. But it was one he could remember for a lifetime. It set up a TD that came a few plays later.

The fourth quarter brought the last of the three important passes. But it was not thrown by Starr. Rather, it was a desperation heave by Raider quarterback Daryle Lamonica. He was trying to play catch-up ball. Packer cornerback Herb Adderley charged in front of the receiver on Green Bay's 40. He made the interception. He raced along the sideline. Sixty yards later, Herb was across the goal line.

Super Bowl II ended 33–14 in favor of the Packers. They had back-to-back wins in the championship battle. Again, the NFL had downed the AFL.

Again, the veteran Packers were the best in the nation.

The win meant a great deal to Vince Lombardi. He was retiring as coach. He had a new job with Green Bay's front office. His team had given him a wonderful victory for his final game.

SUPER BOWL III
NEW YORK JETS (AFL)
vs.
BALTIMORE COLTS (NFL)

Hardly anyone thought the New York Jets had a chance on Sunday, January 12, 1969. After all, the AFL hadn't yet taken a Super Bowl win. Both victories had been solid ones for the NFL. Maybe the AFL teams just weren't strong enough for the competition.

This kind of thinking angered Joe Namath, New York's 25-year-old quarterback. Joe had been a star at the University of Alabama. He'd been with the Jets four years. This past 1968 season, he had led them to an 11–3 record (11 wins–3 losses). Joe had gotten them into Super Bowl III by edging Oakland 27–23 for the AFL crown.

His Jets were good. He felt they would do well. In fact, Namath was *sure* they would do well. He had some cocky words for the press before the game. He told a reporter, "I think we'll win. In fact, I'll guarantee it."

Fans and sportswriters across the country grinned. Yes, Joe was a fine passer. But he was taking the Jets against the Baltimore Colts. The Colts were a powerhouse outfit. They had a 13–1 record for the 1968 season. They'd blanked Cleveland 34–0 to claim the NFL title. How could New York handle such power? The Colts were favored to take the game by about three touchdowns.

Then Namath said something else. He said that Baltimore quarterback Earl Morrall was a long way from being the best in pro ball. Joe thought there were "four or five quarterbacks in our league" who were better than Morrall.

The Colt fans were furious! Morrall was backup man for the great Johnny Unitas. Johnny had been hit by a sore elbow early in the season. So Earl had replaced him. Earl had done a fine job. He had the NFL crown and the trip to Super Bowl III to prove it.

At kickoff time, there were 75,377 fans in the Orange Bowl. They were ready to see the angry Colts batter the underdog Jets!

At first, the game looked as if it *would* be a battering. The Jets took the opening kickoff. They weren't able to get past their own 40 on a series of running plays. Then a punt sent the ball to Baltimore's 27. Morrall went right to work.

First, he fired over the middle to tight end John Mackey for 19 yards. Next, he sent halfback Tom Matte on a sweep for 10 yards. Then Matte shared the carrying honors with fullback Jerry Hill for some more yardage. Finally, Morrall arced the ball to wide receiver Tom Mitchell for 15 yards. The Colts were at New York's 19.

The crowd was delighted. They looked forward to seeing the first TD of the day.

But not yet. The Jets' defense stiffened on the next plays. Baltimore failed to get a first down. Lou Michaels came in for a field goal attempt. With his accuracy, the 3 points promised to be a cinch. Somehow, though, he drove the ball wide of the uprights.

The watching fans were surprised. But they weren't worried. The game was still going to be a battering. So Baltimore had missed a chance to score. So what? There would be another one very soon.

They were right. It came late in the first quarter. The Jets were pinned down on their own 4 after a punt. Joe Namath risked a bullet pass to wide receiver George Sauer. Sauer made the reception. But he was hit hard by defensive back Lenny Lyles. The ball popped out of his hands and went bounc-

*Joe Namath of the New York Jets spots
a receiver late in Super Bowl III.
Jumping high for an attempted pass block
is Bubba Smith of the Baltimore Colts.*

ing along the turf. Linebacker Ron Porter threw himself on it. The Colts had possession. They were less than 20 yards from the goal line.

Here it comes, the crowd thought. The first score of the day, for sure this time.

Baltimore drove to the 13 as the quarter ended. Morrall opened the second period by taking the snap and turning left. He stepped back and began looking for receivers. He saw tight end Tom Mitchell in the end zone. He released the ball. But Jet linebacker Al Atkinson moved into its path. Al jumped with his right arm outstretched. His fingers touched the ball, flicking it high. It came down just behind Mitchell, hit his shoulder pads, and shot high again. It sailed right to defensive back Randy Beverly for a touchback.

The fans were shocked. Twice in a row, they'd seen the mighty Colts fail to score. They were even more shocked in the next minutes. The Jets took possession. Namath gave the ball to fullback Matt Snell on a series of four running plays. Matt slammed his way to his 46. He would rush for 121 yards by day's end.

At that point, Namath went to the air. The Colts tried their famous pass rush on him. But Joe wasn't about to be stopped. He released the ball with lightning speed before the tacklers could get to him. Halfback Bill Mathis made the reception for a 6-yard gain into Baltimore territory. Joe picked George Sauer as his next target. Lenny Lyles almost knocked the ball down. But it thudded into George's chest. He was finally dumped on the 23.

Next, a run picked up another 2 yards. Then Namath threw short to Matt Snell. Matt put his head down and plowed to the 9. Then he took a hand-off. The fullback bulled to the 4 behind the blocking of right guard Randy Rasmussen.

The Orange Bowl was filled with thunder. The fans had started to pull for New York. They couldn't help themselves. Joe Namath was proving that he was a great quarterback. The Jets weren't taking a beating. They were *giving* a beating!

Once again, Namath handed off to Snell. The fullback plunged toward the left side of the line. Tackle Winston Hill and guard Bob Talamini opened a hole for him. Teammate Emerson Boozer cut down safetyman Rick Volk. Snell crashed through the line. Linebacker Dennis Gaubatz came charging in. Snell muscled him out of the way and threw himself at the goal line. When he hit the ground, he was in the end zone.

At last, the crowd had seen a touchdown. But by the underdog Jets, not the bruising Colts!

The AFL team was ahead! It was a first in the short history of the Super Bowl. Jim Turner took care of the PAT. He made the score 7–0.

The Colts fought hard to even things up. Twice, they came within scoring range. They failed to post a tally both times. First, Lou Michaels missed another field goal. Then Earl Morrall tossed a 15-yard pass to the end zone. It was intercepted.

The Jets were red hot when they started the second half. Soon after kicking off, they recovered a Baltimore fumble. They brought Jim Turner in for a 32-yard field goal. The ball sailed neatly between the uprights. New York's lead went to 10–0.

Baltimore was as cold as the Jets were hot. The Colts couldn't move the ball on their downs and had to punt. Then they couldn't keep Namath from driving to their 23.

By now, the Colts were in a fury. They saw Joe drop back to pass. Defensive tackle Fred Miller shot through the line. He came at Joe like an express train. For once, Namath couldn't avoid the tackle. Just as he released the ball, Miller slammed into him. The pass fell short. Joe and Miller hit the ground. A pain shot through Joe's throwing hand. His thumb had been jammed.

Namath headed for the sidelines. All eyes in the Orange Bowl were on him. Was the Jet quarterback seriously hurt and out of the game for good? If so, could the Colts change the tide of battle?

Babe Parilli, Joe's backup man, took over. He failed to move the ball against a toughening defense. Once more, Jim Turner came in for a field goal try. And, once more, he neatly cut the uprights. The score changed to 13–0.

Namath wasn't the only starting quarterback on the bench. Desperate to catch up, the Colts removed Earl Morrall. The quarterback had brought them to the Super Bowl. Morrall watched silently as Johnny Unitas — with his elbow still sore — took command. Johnny had been an inspiring player throughout his career. Now he had to save the day for the Colts.

But he did no better than Morrall on the first series of plays. The Jets stopped him cold. Baltimore was forced to punt. The quarter ended.

Namath's injury, though painful, was not serious. The crowd thundered its approval when he returned to the game in the third period. They went on thundering in the fourth period. The Jets passed and rushed to Baltimore's 2 before being stopped. Jim Turner kicked his third field goal of the day. The thunder became deafening.

16–0!

It was amazing! New York was supposed to lose by about three touchdowns. But Baltimore needed three TDs just to catch up. The Jets were turning the game into a rout. They might even blank the mighty Colts.

Johnny Unitas was in no mood for a blanking.

Showing the leadership that had made him famous, he got his team moving. He connected with passes for 5, 7, and 5 yards. Tom Matte made a fine 19-yard dash. Then a 12-yard run by Jerry Hill brought the Colts to the Jets' 25.

Unitas wanted a fast 6 points. He dropped back to pass. His wide receiver, Jimmy Orr, broke into the clear at the goal line. Johnny fired the ball. Defensive back Randy Beverly closed in on Orr while the pass was in the air. The two men fought for the ball —and Randy came away with it!

The Baltimore fans groaned. Once again, their Colts had missed a score.

But the Colts were not to be denied at least one TD. They stopped a New York drive deep into their own territory. Then they moved steadily downfield on a series of passes and runs. It brought them 80 yards to the Jet 1. From there, running back Jerry Hill plunged into the end zone. A successful PAT made the score 16–7.

There were now just over 3 minutes left to play. If they were to score again, the Colts had to regain possession fast. They tried an onside kick on the kickoff. The trick worked. The ball skipped off George Sauer and bounced along the ground. Players went at it from all directions. Baltimore's Tom Mitchell ended up with it.

Once more, Unitas put his throwing arm to

work. The Colts moved quickly to New York's 19. There, the Jets held them. On fourth down, Johnny uncorked a desperation pass to Jimmy Orr. Linebacker Randy Grantham raced over and knocked it down. Another scoring attempt had failed.

It was the last gasp of the day for Baltimore. The clock showed 2:21 when the Jets took over. Namath locked the game away by eating up the time with running plays.

Only 8 seconds were left by the time Baltimore regained possession. The stadium echoed with the roar of the crowd as they counted down the seconds. The biggest upset in the short history of the Super Bowl went into the books.

Everyone remembered Joe Namath's words before the game. Everyone had thought that he had a big mouth. But now he had a 16–7 win to his credit. He'd made a promise. And he'd kept it.

Super Bowl III was a critical one for the AFL. Before the game, there had been talk of ending the Super Bowl battles. They'd end if the American League representative didn't play better football.

That sort of talk was never to be heard again. The Jets had proven that the AFL was strong enough for the competition. The next years would see even stronger AFL teams in the Super Bowl.

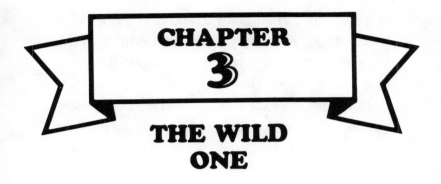

CHAPTER 3

THE WILD ONE

Joe Namath closed the 1960s with some great Super Bowl moments. The 1970s started with some that were just as great.

SUPER BOWL IV
KANSAS CITY CHIEFS (AFL)
vs.
MINNESOTA VIKINGS (NFL)

Super Bowl IV was played at New Orleans on January 11, 1970. It was a game that Kansas City kicker Jan Stenerud would never forget.

In the first quarter, his Chiefs battled a short distance into Viking territory. Then they were stopped. Jan trotted in for a field goal try. Kicking soccer style, he calmly split the uprights. They were 48 yards away! It was the longest field goal ever seen in Super Bowl play.

Jan's kick gave the Chiefs a 3–0 lead. He posted two more successful field goals before the day was done. One shot traveled 32 yards. The other went 25 yards.

The Chiefs walked off with a 23–7 victory. They more than made up for their loss to Green Bay in Super Bowl I. For a second time, an AFL team had taken the championship.

Super Bowl IV marked the last such meeting between the AFL and NFL. In the weeks following the game, the final details of the AFL-NFL merger were completed. The *new* National Football League came into being. The AFL joined it as the American Football Conference. The old NFL became the National Football Conference.

Each conference was split into three divisions: the Eastern, Central, and Western Divisions. The teams were assigned to the divisions as shown on the facing page.

Three old NFL outfits were placed in the AFC. They were the Baltimore Colts, the Cleveland Browns, and the Pittsburgh Steelers. This gave an equal number of teams to each conference. Then,

NATIONAL FOOTBALL CONFERENCE (NFC)

Eastern
Dallas Cowboys
New York Giants
St. Louis Cardinals
Washington Redskins
Philadelphia Eagles

Central
Minnesota Vikings
Detroit Lions
Chicago Bears
Green Bay Packers

Western
San Francisco 49ers
Los Angeles Rams
Atlanta Falcons
New Orleans Saints

AMERICAN FOOTBALL CONFERENCE (AFC)

Eastern
Baltimore Colts
Miami Dolphins
New York Jets
Buffalo Bills
Boston Patriots

Central
Cincinnati Bengals
Cleveland Browns
Pittsburgh Steelers
Houston Oilers

Western
Oakland Raiders
Kansas City Chiefs
San Diego Chargers
Denver Broncos

a few years later, the conferences were expanded. In 1976, the Seattle Seahawks became a member of the NFC's Western Division. The Tampa Bay Buccaneers joined the Western Division of the AFC. One year later, Tampa and Seattle switched conferences. Today, Seattle is in the AFC West. Tampa Bay is in the NFC Central Division.

Each conference was to hold a series of playoff games at the end of each season. The teams that had won the division championships in their conference, plus a "wild-card" team, would play. (The wild card is the team with the next best record.) The playoffs would produce a champion for each conference. The conference champs would then meet in the Super Bowl to decide the national title.

The Dallas Cowboys came out of the 1970 season as the NFC champions. They beat the San Francisco 49ers 17–10 in the final playoff game. Baltimore ended the AFC playoffs with a 27–17 win over the Oakland Raiders. The two conference winners then headed for Miami's Orange Bowl and Super Bowl V.

It was played on Sunday, January 17, 1971, in front of 80,055 screaming fans. The game turned out to be one of the wildest Super Bowl battles ever seen. It had everything — strange plays, a hair-raising finish, and so many mistakes that the sportswriters dubbed it "the Blooper Bowl."

SUPER BOWL V
BALTIMORE COLTS (AFC)
vs.
DALLAS COWBOYS (NFC)

The mistakes started to crop up right away. Baltimore had the ball. Working in his own territory, quarterback Johnny Unitas tried a pass. The ball got away from him. It thudded into the arms of Cowboy linebacker Chuck Howley. Chuck headed downfield for 22 yards before the Colts reached him. Luckily for the Colts, the interception cost them nothing. Dallas went nowhere on the next plays.

The interception was an embarrassing one for Unitas. But Cowboy quarterback Craig Morton was even more red-faced a few minutes later. After leading his team to the Colt 7-yard line, Craig whipped a pass into the end zone. He delivered the ball too high. It sailed far above his leaping receiver. The chance for a TD was lost. Dallas had to settle for a field goal and a 3–0 lead.

Craig was in for more trouble. In the second quarter, the Cowboys again pushed deep into Baltimore territory. This time, they reached the 7. Once more, Craig tried a pass. But he threw to the wrong man — an ineligible receiver! Another TD was missed. Dallas took a 15-yard penalty for intentional grounding. They couldn't get back to the goal line. They settled for another field goal. It increased their lead to 6–0.

So far, Dallas had made two mistakes. That put them one blooper ahead. So the Colts decided to even things up. But they turned their goof into a score.

The fun started on the Colt 23. Johnny Unitas stepped back to pass. Wide receiver Eddie Hinton cut in from the sideline. Johnny threw down the middle to him. The pass was weak and high. Eddie jumped for it. The ball touched his fingers and sailed away. Defensive back Mel Renfro dashed over, hoping to intercept. He managed to get a hand on the ball. But it got away again! It went straight to Baltimore's John Mackey.

The big tight end was surprised. But he didn't let the ball escape. Mackey pulled it in and headed downfield. The Cowboys chased him for 45 yards. They never caught him. The score was now tied 6–6. It stayed that way when the try for PAT was blocked.

Then came another wild moment. Baltimore had the ball on its own 29. Johnny Unitas took the snap. Linebacker Lee Roy Jordan charged through the line and slammed into him. Johnny went down hard. The ball popped out of his hands. There was a scramble of fighting players. Finally, the mess cleared. Cowboy defensive tackle Jethro Pugh lay on the ground, clutching the ball.

Johnny's fumble opened the way for a Dallas score. The Cowboys made it to the Colt 7. There, Craig Morton tried another end zone pass. No blooper occurred this time. The ball went right to Duane Thomas. He divided his time between the halfback and fullback spots. A successful PAT moved the Cowboys ahead 13–6.

There was more trouble for Johnny Unitas on the Colts' next possession. He was hit hard by defensive end George Andrie on a pass play. The pass was intercepted by Herb Adderley. And Johnny was out of the game with injured ribs.

The mistakes popped up again as soon as the third quarter started. The Colts took the opening kickoff. They charged upfield and fumbled on the tackle at their 31. Dallas recovered.

Craig Morton's troops moved to the Colt 2 on the next five plays. They seemed certain to widen their lead. Morton now called for a run. He handed off to Duane Thomas. Head down and knees driving, Thomas charged for the end zone. He got as far as the 1-foot line. Tacklers crashed into him. The ball shot out of his hands. A Colt threw himself on it.

For the third time, Dallas had missed a TD!

But the Colts weren't about to let Dallas make *all* the mistakes. It was quarterback Earl Morrall's turn to goof. Morrall, remember, had put in such a bad day in Super Bowl III. Now he was in for the injured Unitas. He led the way deep into Dallas territory. Then he fired a pass to the goal line. The throw was a good one. But Morrall groaned. It was Super Bowl III all over again. A Cowboy defender cut in front of the receiver and grabbed the ball. Linebacker Chuck Howley had made his second interception of the day. He would be named the game's Most Valuable Player. Howley was the only player from a losing team ever named MVP in Super Bowl history.

The players thought they had made enough mistakes. But there were more to come. In the fourth quarter, Dallas was trying to move upfield from its own 23. Craig Morton risked a short pass to fullback Walt Garrison. The ball bounced off Garrison's fingers. Colt safetyman Rick Volk reached up, got his hands on the ball, and held on.

Instantly, he was heading down the sideline. The end zone came closer and closer. He could hear tacklers pounding in on him. At last, he reached the 3-yard line. He went no farther.

It was a nice stop by Dallas. But it couldn't keep

Baltimore from scoring. Moments later, running back Tom Nowatzke plunged over for the TD. The PAT was good. With 7:35 left to play, the score stood tied at 13–13!

It was time for the game's hair-raising finish. Dallas received the kickoff and was downed immediately. The Cowboys tried to get upfield with some running plays. The Colts stopped them with a vicious defense. The clock worked its way down to 1:09. The Cowboys were still a long way from midfield. Were the fans in for the first overtime action in Super Bowl history? Morton *had* to come up with a quick TD. He decided he had to pass. Here came the final blooper of the day.

Craig pedaled back. His teammates blocked hard for him. He released the ball. But Colt linebacker Mike Curtis snatched it for the interception at the Dallas 41! Curtis plowed his way to the 28.

The game was as good as over. The Colts used two rushes to run the clock down to 9 seconds. Then they brought in kicker Jim O'Brien for a 32-yard field goal try. The watching fans held their breath. O'Brien was a rookie. Would he be able to make a game-winning kick? Or, would he make the final blooper? Would he miss and send the game into overtime?

The Cowboys hurled insults at Jim. They wanted

to rattle him as he took his position. But he paid them no attention. Head down, he watched the ball as it was snapped to the holder. He stepped forward. He swung his leg smoothly. The ball was up and sailing. And then, O'Brien's arms were stretched overhead in triumph. He was jumping high as the ball sailed between the uprights.

Super Bowl V was over. It had been the first played under the new National Football League. It had been the wildest one the fans had seen. It belonged to the Baltimore Colts, 16–13.

A wall of Dallas Cowboys
rises in front of rookie
kicker Jim O'Brien as he
tries a 32-yard field goal
in the final seconds of
Super Bowl V.
The kick was good
and gave the Baltimore
Colts a 16–13 win.
Quarterback Earl Morrall
holds for O'Brien.

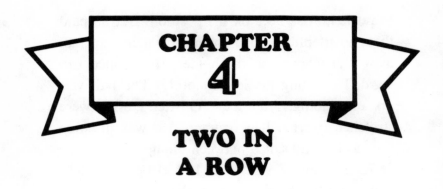

CHAPTER 4

TWO IN
A ROW

The 1970s had started in a wild way. Top Super Bowl action continued throughout the decade.

SUPER BOWL VI
DALLAS COWBOYS (NFC)
vs.
MIAMI DOLPHINS (AFC)

Dallas linebacker Chuck Howley had won the MVP award in Super Bowl V. Now he and the Cowboys were in New Orleans for Super Bowl VI. It was January 16, 1972. Howley was due for another great moment in his career.

It came in the fourth quarter when Miami was

trailing 17–3. During a hard drive, Dolphin quarterback Bob Griese tried a pass to halfback Jim Kiick at midfield. Chuck Howley was knocked to the ground as the play opened. He saw Kiick breaking into the clear for the reception. Howley jumped to his feet. He raced over to cover as the pass was released.

Chuck weighed 225 pounds (101 kg), but he moved fast. He reached Kiick and swerved in front of him. The ball pounded into the linebacker's hands. He held on and started downfield. Tacklers came at him. He saw silver-helmeted blockers cut them down. Chalk lines swept by underfoot. Chuck covered 41 yards before he was hit at the Dolphin 9.

Chuck had hoped the run would end in a TD. He hadn't scored, but he was still a happy man. His interception set up the final tally for the day. A pass to tight end Mike Ditka gave Dallas a 24–3 win over Miami.

It was the first Super Bowl victory for the Cowboys. And it was a first for their new number-one quarterback, Roger Staubach. He had worked behind Craig Morton since 1969. He was destined to become one of the finest players in the pro ranks. And the Cowboys were destined to return to the Super Bowl many times.

SUPER BOWL VII
MIAMI DOLPHINS (AFC)
vs.
WASHINGTON REDSKINS (NFC)

They had scored only 3 points in Super Bowl VI. (It was the least ever posted in the championship battles.) But Coach Don Shula's Dolphins promised themselves a solid win when they came to Super Bowl VII. It was held in Los Angeles on January 14, 1973. The Dolphins kept their promise, downing the Washington Redskins 14–7.

They also gave the 90,182 fans in the Memorial Coliseum the funniest moment in Super Bowl history. It happened just 2 minutes before the end of the game. The Dolphins were leading 14–0. They were on the brink of posting the Super Bowl's first shutout.

Cowboy linebacker Chuck Howley
swerved in front of Jim Kiick
to make an interception
at midfield in Super Bowl VI.
Chuck then raced 41 yards
before he was brought down
at the Miami Dolphins' 9.

They were also close to another tally. The ball was on Washington's 34. The Dolphins' attack had been stalled there. In came stubby Garo Yepremian for a field goal try. A fine kicker, he'd helped Miami to its perfect 14–0 record for the regular season. Everyone was sure he could add 3 points to the score. The kick was a cinch at this distance.

But Washington staged a hard rush. Redskin left tackle Bill Brundige jumped high and knocked the ball down. It hit the turf and bounded back toward Garo. He chased after the ball and scooped it up. Then, with giant tacklers closing in fast, he headed for the sidelines. All he wanted was to get safely out of bounds.

Suddenly, Garo changed his mind. He couldn't play it safe after all. The tacklers were coming too fast. They seemed sure to get him for a big loss. He spotted a receiver. Garo made a fine living as a kicker. Now he decided to become a passer.

Back went his arm as he ran. Forward it came. Oops! The ball slipped out of his fingers. The pass went wild. The crowd jumped up. They watched the ball wobble through the air. It flopped into the arms of Mike Bass.

There was just one problem. Mike wasn't a Dolphin. He played right cornerback for Washington.

Mike made the catch on the Miami 49-yard line.

He had a clear field to the end zone. Tucking the ball in, he started to run. He heard a roar coming from the stands. And he heard the Dolphins pounding behind him. He showed all the speed that he had. No one could touch him. Mike shot across the goal line.

It was a play that made headlines everywhere. But the Dolphins didn't think it was funny. It cost them the first shutout in Super Bowl history. They had to settle for a 14–7 victory.

The Dolphins were disappointed at missing the shutout. But they weren't too disappointed. How could they be? They hadn't had a single defeat all season. And they had topped everything off by taking the championship. They were the first team in the new National Football League to play a perfect season.

They were in for even more glory.

SUPER BOWL VIII
MIAMI DOLPHINS (AFC)
vs.
MINNESOTA VIKINGS (NFC)

So far, the Green Bay Packers were said to be the best of the Super Bowl teams. They had made two trips to the championship battle. So had Baltimore, Kansas City, Dallas, and Miami. But the Pack had won both their games. And they had won them back to back.

Now, as 1974 dawned, the Dolphins were about to better Green Bay's record in one way. They were headed for Houston and Super Bowl VIII. They were to become the first team ever to compete in three Super Bowls. And they had a chance to match Green Bay's record of back-to-back wins.

Miami fans across the country wanted to see Coach Don Shula take Super Bowl VIII. They knew how much he admired Green Bay's former coach, the late Vince Lombardi. They also knew that he was a coach much like Lombardi. Miami had been a losing team when Don took it over four years ago. He had turned the Dolphins into winners through lots of hard work. Lombardi had done the same thing with Green Bay years ago.

Wouldn't it be great if Shula could match the back-to-back wins of a man he admired so much?

The Dolphins were favored to win Super Bowl VIII by a slight margin. Actually, it promised to be anybody's game. The Dolphins were going against Coach Bud Grant's Minnesota Vikings. The Vikings boasted one of the best quarterbacks in the business. He was the scrambling Fran Tarkenton. And they had a top-notch defense nicknamed "the Purple People Eaters."

Both teams had identical 12–2 records for the 1973 season. Both had won their conference championships by beating tough teams. Miami had downed the Oakland Raiders. Minnesota had knocked over Dallas. The scores of the two games had been the same: 27–10.

So who would claim the crown?

The 68,142 fans in Houston's Rice Stadium wondered. It was a cold and drizzly day. Miami's Jake Scott took the opening kickoff at his own 7. He streaked for 31 yards before the Vikes finally downed him. Then quarterback Bob Griese called a series of running plays that drove Minnesota wild. Time after time, he handed off to backs Larry Csonka and Mercury Morris. They rushed for solid gains. Hard blocking knocked the Purple People Eaters out of the way.

The drive lasted for ten plays. It carried the Dolphins to Minnesota's 5. Once again, Griese handed off to Csonka. Up in the line, guards Bob Kuechenberg and Larry Little pulled to the right. The Vikes went with them. They thought the run was going in that direction. But Csonka headed left against the flow. He saw daylight in the line. He turned, plunged through, and hurled himself into the end zone. The Dolphins had a 6-point lead. Garo Yepremian kicked the PAT to make it 7–0.

The drive and the TD had eaten up more than 5 minutes of playing time. The Miami offense had been the stars so far. Now the Miami defense took over. Hitting hard, they stopped Minnesota's first series of plays cold. They swarmed over Fran Tarkenton when he tried to pass. They charged through the line and chopped down the running attempts. The Vikes were able to gain only 9 yards. They were forced to punt.

Back onto the field came the Miami offense. Griese tried a combination of passes and runs. They worked. The Dolphins were on Minnesota's 14, with just 2 minutes left in the quarter. Griese fired a short pass to wide receiver Marlin Briscoe. Marlin made the reception. He was dropped at the 1-yard line.

The Vikes now expected a running play — and they got one. The ball went from Griese to halfback Jim Kiick. Jim put his head down. He hit the middle of the line. He threw himself forward and landed in the end zone. Garo Yepremian's PAT set the score at 14–0.

Then the Vikings got tough. The game turned into a seesaw battle in the second quarter. Neither team gained much ground. The Dolphins, however, managed to put another tally on the board. Garo Yepremian stretched their lead to 17–0 with

Miami's Larry Csonka bursts through the line to score the first touchdown in Super Bowl VIII.

a 28-yard field goal. He had made up for his funny goof in Super Bowl VII.

By now, the Vikings had had enough. John Gilliam took the kickoff at the start of the third quarter. He charged downfield. His blockers took care of the first tacklers. Then, he shifted into high gear. He swept past a string of Dolphins on his own. He crossed the midfield stripe. The crowd was on its feet. Could he go the whole way? No! He was finally pulled down. But the return had been for 65 yards. It was just the spark the Vikes needed.

Then the Minnesota fans groaned. There was a yellow handkerchief on the turf back near the Viking goal. The referee was signaling a clip. He was pointing to Minnesota tight end Stu Voight. The run had been for nothing! The ball came back to the Viking 11.

The penalty seemed to kill that spark. The Vikings couldn't manage a first down on the next plays. They punted.

Miami took possession on Minnesota's 43. Morris and Csonka rushed for short gains. Then came the top play of the series — and perhaps the game. Bob Griese went to the pocket, pumped, and fired to wide receiver Paul Warfield. The ball went wide. Warfield threw himself at it. He stretched himself out flat in a dive. He hit the ground with the ball in his arms. The catch gave Miami a 27-yard gain. The next plays took the Dolphins to Minnesota's 2.

Again, Griese called on Larry Csonka. The big back took the handoff. Crashing ahead, he found running room. He plunged into the end zone for his second TD. After Yepremian's PAT, the scoreboard read 24–0.

Were the fans about to see a miracle? The Dolphins were on the brink of back-to-back wins. They were also close to a shutout. They had just missed one last year. Could they post one today? It seemed impossible in tough Super Bowl competition.

It was. Fran Tarkenton wasn't about to see his team shamed by a scoreless day. He finally got a Viking drive going. For the first time in the game, he brought the ball near to the Miami goalposts. Then, as the fourth quarter opened, Fran kept the ball on a running play. He streaked into the end zone. At last, the Vikes were on the scoreboard. After the PAT, they trailed 24–7.

Then they set out to close things up even more. On the kickoff, they tried an onside kick. It seemed to work. The ball bounced off a Dolphin and went to a Viking. But a penalty nullified the play. Miami took over and played a scoreless final quarter.

So, the Dolphins had their back-to-back wins. Don Shula had matched Vince Lombardi's record. And, of course, he had a new record all his own. Of all the NFL teams, only his Dolphins had three Super Bowls to their credit.

And another record had been set that day. It belonged to Larry Csonka. The big back had posted 145 yards on 33 carries. The old record belonged to Matt Snell of the Jets. He'd posted 121 yards in Super Bowl III.

All the records were great ones. But they would soon be broken. The winning years of the Pittsburgh Steelers were about to dawn. The Steelers were to play in four of the next six Super Bowl games.

CHAPTER 5

THE QUARTER THAT HAD EVERYTHING

The Steelers posted a 10–3–1 record for the 1974 season. Then they beat Oakland 24–13 for the AFC crown. They headed to New Orleans for Super Bowl IX. On Sunday, January 12, 1975, they found themselves in a game that had a very odd moment.

SUPER BOWL IX
PITTSBURGH STEELERS (AFC)
vs.
MINNESOTA VIKINGS (NFC)

A star quarterback isn't supposed to tally a score for the opposition. But that's what Fran Tarkenton did in the second quarter.

The game was scoreless. The Vikings were on their own 10-yard line. Fran took the snap. He turned for a pitchout to one of his backs. But the throw got away from him. He missed his man. Fran saw the ball bounce across the turf and tumble into the end zone.

And he saw the Steeler linemen go chasing after it. If they got to it, Pittsburgh would have a TD. Instantly, Fran threw himself across the goal line. He hit the ground. The ball thumped against his ribs. He wrapped his arms around it. Then Steeler white shirts were landing on him.

Fran knew that he had scored a safety — 2 points for the opposition. It was bad. But not as bad as a touchdown. At least, he'd saved his Vikes 4 points.

Pittsburgh went on to a 16–6 win, their first Super Bowl victory. The Vikings went home with a frustrating record. They and the Dolphins were the only teams to have played in three Super Bowls so far. But, unlike the Dolphins, they hadn't yet managed a win.

The Steelers were delighted with the day. It had been a record-breaking one for running back Franco Harris. He had bettered Larry Csonka's rushing mark of last year. Franco had carried 34 times for 158 yards. That gave him an average of 4.6 yards per carry.

And quarterback Terry Bradshaw was a happy man. Many fans and sportswriters had said he wasn't talented enough to lead a team to the Super Bowl. Well, he'd proved them wrong, especially in the final quarter. He had masterminded a 66-yard drive that ended in a 4-yard TD pass to tight end Larry Brown. It was the tally that put the game on ice for Pittsburgh.

Terry would soon prove again that he had the stuff to lead a championship team.

SUPER BOWL X
PITTSBURGH STEELERS (AFC)
vs.
DALLAS COWBOYS (NFC)

Terry and the Steelers came to Super Bowl X after beating Oakland 16–10 for the AFC crown. It was the second year in a row they had downed the West Coast team in playoff action. Their record for the 1975 season stood at 12–2.

Facing them were the Dallas Cowboys. They had put in a 10–4 season. The Cowboys had gone into the NFC playoffs as the wild card team. In the final seconds of the first game, Roger Staubach heaved a 50-yard TD bomb to wide receiver Drew Pearson. It edged out Minnesota 17–14. The Cowboys then walloped the Los Angeles Rams 37–7 to take the conference crown. Dallas became the first wild card team to reach the Super Bowl.

Super Bowl X was played in Miami on January 18, 1976. Many sports reporters felt that it was one of the best championship battles ever. They singled out the fourth quarter as being especially exciting. It was, they said, the quarter that "had everything."

Actually, there was plenty of excitement right from the start. The 80,197 fans in the Orange Bowl were really entertained. Just 4 minutes into the first quarter, Roger Staubach faded back to pass. Wide receiver Drew Pearson ran a crossing pattern over the middle. Roger put the ball right on target. Drew made the reception without breaking stride. The play was good for 29 yards and a TD. The PAT gave Dallas a 7–0 lead.

Pittsburgh quarterback Terry Bradshaw is determined to release the ball. Dallas defensive end Ed "Too Tall" Jones is just as determined to bring him down.

But the score didn't stay that way for long. The Steelers started moving on their own 33 after the kickoff. They drove across midfield on rushes by backs Franco Harris and Rocky Bleier. Then Terry Bradshaw sent wide receiver Lynn Swann racing down the sideline. Terry stepped into the pocket and threw the ball high to him.

The Cowboys' left cornerback, Mark Washington, was covering Swann. Both men jumped for the ball. But Swann sailed high above Washington. He looked like a long-legged bird in flight. He grabbed the ball for a 32-yard gain. It was the first of three fine catches that Lynn would make that day. Minutes later, Bradshaw aimed a 7-yard bullet at tight end Randy Grossman in the end zone. Roy Gerela's PAT tied things at 7–7.

The fireworks continued. In the second period, kicker Toni Fritsch put Dallas ahead 10–7 with a 36-yard field goal. Next, Bradshaw sailed the ball 53 yards to Lynn Swann. Lynn posted his second great reception of the day. It left the fans gasping. To make the catch, Lynn had to throw himself at the ball. He got his hands on it and juggled it for a split second. Then, he pulled it in and went tumbling along the ground. The catch set up a field goal try for Roy Gerela. But Roy missed.

He missed on yet another try in the third period.

The score remained 10–7 through the quarter. Then came the quarter that "had everything." It all started about 2 minutes into the period.

The Cowboys had the ball. Their backs were against their own goal line. The snap went to Mitch Hoopes for a punt. Mitch stepped forward and swung his leg. Pittsburgh fullback Reggie Harrison slammed through the line. He threw himself at the ball just as it was kicked. It hit him full in the face mask. The ball bounded across the end zone and shot out of bounds.

Twice in two years, the fans had seen something rare — a safety. The Steelers had closed the score to 10–9.

They pushed into the lead less than 3 minutes later. Terry Bradshaw engineered a running and passing drive to the Dallas 20. It stalled there. Roy Gerela came in for a field goal try. The Pittsburgh fans crossed their fingers. Roy wasn't having a good afternoon. He'd already missed two shots. But he was determined not to miss another time. The ball sailed neatly between the uprights. The score was 12–10 for the Steelers.

In another 2 minutes, the Steelers had the Cowboys pinned down on their own 15. Roger Staubach dropped back almost to the goal line. He pumped and sent the ball toward Drew Pearson.

Pittsburgh safetyman Mike Wagner saw the play coming. He headed for Pearson.

But he was careful to stay just out of the wide receiver's view. Then, in the last second, he lunged in front of Drew. He snatched the ball on the run! Wagner set off down the sideline like an express train. Dallas managed to nail him at the 7.

The Cowboy defense played hard. They kept the Steelers from getting any closer on the next plays. Roy Gerela trotted in for his fourth field goal try. He evened his score for the day to 2–2 on a solid kick. The Pittsburgh lead was stretched to 15–10.

The game now seesawed back and forth for a few minutes. Then there were just under 4 minutes left to play. The Steelers had the ball on their own 36. They were looking at a third-and-four situation. Terry Bradshaw knew that he had to pass. He decided to try a bomb — a play called 69 Maximum Flanker Post.

At the snap, Lynn Swann streaked down the sideline. He moved like a rocket. Terry Bradshaw dropped back. His backfield men started to form a pocket for him. But the Cowboys smelled pass. They blitzed. Linebacker D. D. Lewis came charging at Terry. Storming right behind Lewis was right safetyman Cliff Harris. Terry didn't see them. They were on his blind side.

Bradshaw was looking for his receiver. He found him. The quarterback pumped. Would the charging Lewis get to him before the release? D. D. threw himself at Terry. But Terry must have sensed that he was there. The quarterback took a quick step to his right. Lewis sailed harmlessly past.

Now Terry's arm went back and shot forward. The pass was away. Just as the ball left Terry's hand, Harris crashed into him. Leather slammed into leather. The two men went down hard.

Bradshaw lay half conscious on the turf. He didn't see where the pass went. But the fans did. They screamed as the ball sailed far downfield. They saw Swann racing along the sideline. They saw Dallas cornerback Mark Washington trying to keep up with him. They saw the ball dropping toward the Dallas 5. They saw Lynn go up high for it. They saw it disappear into his arms. . .

And they saw him flash across the goal line!

From the line of scrimmage, the pass was good for 59 yards. Swann made it into a 64-yard scoring play by dashing the last 5 yards to the goal line. Terry had dropped far back for the throw. The ball had traveled at least 70 yards in the air!

It was a marvelous throw — and a marvelous catch. The Steelers were now ahead 21–10. The

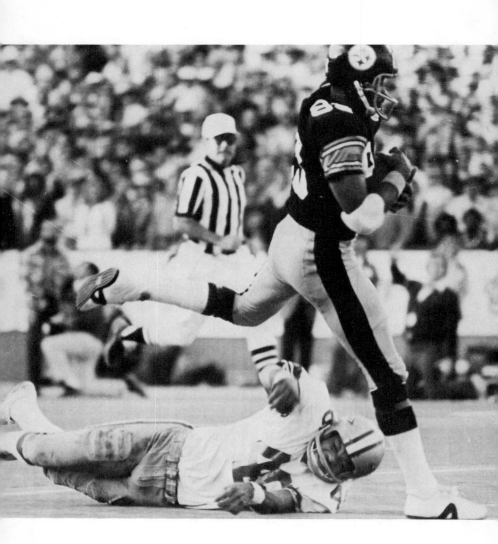

*Lynn Swann gathers in the ball at the
Dallas 5-yard line and streaks
past Mark Washington for the TD.*

score stayed where it was on the PAT. With his bad luck returning, Gerela missed the boot.

Terry Bradshaw was helped from the field. His backup man, Terry Hanratty, took over for him. Bradshaw was still dazed. His mind didn't clear for long minutes. He had set a record for the longest scoring play in Super Bowl history. But he didn't realize it until the game was over and he was back in the Pittsburgh dressing room.

The fans had seen everything that quarter. A safety, two field goals, an interception by Mike Wagner, a sensational pass and catch, and a missed PAT. It was all that any fan could ask for.

But there was more to come. Roger Staubach and the Cowboys started on their own 20 and drove to Pittsburgh's 34 in four plays. Along the way, Roger connected with two fine passes. One went to Drew Pearson for 30 yards. Preston Pearson caught the other. It was good for 11 yards. Then, under a hard rush, Roger sent a 34-yard shot to wide receiver Percy Howard for the TD. The PAT closed the score to 21–17.

Then Pittsburgh took the kickoff. Bradshaw's backup man, Terry Hanratty, was at the controls. The Steelers fought their way to the Dallas 41. There, the Cowboy defense stalled them. It was fourth down with 9 to go. The fans got ready for a punt. But they saw Steeler Coach Chuck Noll call for a run.

It was a risky decision, a real gamble. What if the Cowboys stopped the run? They'd have great field position for a last try at a score. A score could mean winning the game. But Chuck didn't want to give Dallas a chance for a runback on a punt. Further, there was little more than a minute left to play. The Cowboys had used up all their timeouts. If Dallas got the ball, the defense would have to do its best. But if his Steelers made the first down, the game was as good as over.

The gamble didn't pay off. Dallas stopped the running play after a 2-yard gain. The crowd was on its feet. Could Staubach and Pearson pull a miracle out of the hat?

But the quarter with everything was not to see another TD. Dallas tried five plays. The defense swarmed in and stopped them all. The final gun sounded. Super Bowl X belonged to the Pittsburgh Steelers, 21–17.

It was a great victory for the Steelers. They had now joined the Packers and the Dolphins in taking back-to-back wins. And now everyone knew Terry Bradshaw was good enough to lead his team to a championship. He had mixed his plays nicely all day long. He had attempted 19 passes and had completed 9 for a total of 209 yards. Two passes — for 53 yards in the second quarter and for the record-breaking 64 in the fourth — had netted more than 100 of those yards.

For most fans, Lynn Swann had been the *real* star of the game. He had clocked four receptions. Three of them had been the most spectacular catches ever seen in Super Bowl play. Altogether, he had received for a total of 161 yards. It was a Super Bowl record.

And he hadn't been sure he would play at all! Lynn had suffered a concussion in the AFC title match against Oakland. The decision that he was well enough to play in Super Bowl X had been made just minutes before the kickoff.

CHAPTER 6

THE BEST ONE

Pittsburgh won a spot in the AFC playoffs at the end of the 1976 season. But the men in black dropped the conference championship to Oakland 24–7. Gone was the chance to go to Super Bowl XI.

The Steelers were again in the playoffs for the 1977 season. This time, they lost 34–21 to the Denver Broncos in the semifinals.

Denver then edged out the Raiders 20–17 for the conference crown and the trip to Super Bowl XII.

Both Super Bowl XI and XII set records.

SUPER BOWL XI
OAKLAND RAIDERS (AFC)
vs.
MINNESOTA VIKINGS (NFC)

Super Bowl XI drew a record crowd. The game brought 100,421 fans to the Pasadena Rose Bowl on January 9, 1977.

Next, Oakland set a rushing record. The Raiders clocked 266 yards on the ground. The old record belonged to the Dallas Cowboys. They had rushed for 252 yards in Super Bowl VI.

Oakland's biggest gain, however, didn't come on a rush. In the fourth quarter, Minnesota's Fran Tarkenton tried a pass deep into Raider territory. Cornerback Willie Brown intercepted at his own 25. He ran the ball back for 75 yards and a TD.

The Raiders won the game 32–14. It was their first Super Bowl victory. It made up for the 33–14 beating they had taken from Green Bay in Super Bowl II.

For the Vikings, the loss set an unhappy record. They had played in more Super Bowl games than any other team — four in all.

But Minnesota hadn't yet managed to win a single one!

SUPER BOWL XII
DALLAS COWBOYS (NFC)
vs.
DENVER BRONCOS (AFC)

Super Bowl XII was played in the Superdome at New Orleans. It was the first championship battle to be staged indoors.

Many records were set on that January 15, 1978. Most were embarrassing records! Some sportswriters said that XII was the poorest Super Bowl game ever played.

For instance, the game had the most fumbles in Super Bowl history. There were ten in all. Dallas lost the ball six times. Denver gave it away four times.

And the game produced the most penalties. There were 20 for a grand total of 154 yards. Dallas swallowed 12 penalties for 94 yards. Denver lost 60 yards on 8 penalties.

But Super Bowl XII *did* have several great moments.

The best of those were in the fourth quarter. Dallas had the ball on Denver's 29. Roger Staubach took the snap and handed off to running back Robert Newhouse. Newhouse rolled left with the option to pass. As the Broncos charged in on him, he sighted wide receiver Golden Richards in the end zone. Newhouse released a throw. The ball dropped in high. Golden took it with an over-the-head catch for the TD.

The game ended 27–10 for Dallas. Like the Vikings, Tom Landry's Cowboys had now made four trips to the Super Bowl. Unlike the Vikes, they had a win-loss record that stood at 2–2.

SUPER BOWL XIII
PITTSBURGH STEELERS (AFC)
vs.
DALLAS COWBOYS (NFC)

Thirteen is supposed to be an unlucky number. But Super Bowl XIII sure wasn't unlucky for the 78,656 fans in Miami's Orange Bowl. The game was a thriller from start to finish.

Pitted against each other were those old foes from Super Bowl X — the Steelers and the Cowboys. Pittsburgh had downed the Houston Oilers 34–5 for the AFC crown. Dallas took the NFC title with a 28–0 win over the Los Angeles Rams. When the two champions got together on January 21, 1979, they set a new record. They ran the score up to 35–31. It was the highest ever seen in Super Bowl play.

Back in Super Bowl X, Pittsburgh and Dallas had played the final quarter that "had everything." Now the sportswriters said that they did something even better. They played the best and most exciting Super Bowl to date.

The day was rainy. Dallas took the opening kickoff. Halfback Tony Dorsett sprinted through and around the Steeler defense on the first series of plays. He showed the form that had won him the Heisman Trophy in college. Dorsett brought the Cowboys to Pittsburgh's 34. The next play came from Tom Landry on the sideline. It was a double reverse, with the ball finally going to Drew Pearson. But Drew bobbled the wet and slick ball. It hit the ground. Steeler defensive tackle John Banaszak threw himself on it.

Pittsburgh now rushed and passed to the Cowboys' 28. In the huddle, Terry Bradshaw called for "one-eleven-out." The play sent wide receiver John Stallworth racing to the goal line while Terry pedaled back to pass. Stallworth managed to get behind his covering man. Then, the throw came sailing in. He jumped high and came down to dance happily in the end zone. It was the game's first TD. The PAT set the score at 7–0.

The battle seesawed back and forth. There were just seconds left in the quarter. Then Bradshaw fumbled near midfield. Dallas recovered. Three plays later, Staubach connected with a 39-yard shot to wide receiver Tony Hill. It was the final play of the quarter. The Cowboys had scored against the Steelers in the first period. No other team had done that all season long.

The scoreboard showed 7–7 after the PAT. But it soon changed. Dallas burst into the lead on a wild play. Pittsburgh had the ball at the time. Bradshaw moved back to pass near his own 40. He dropped the ball. It was as wet and slippery as ever. But he managed to make the recovery. Then he saw linebackers Thomas "Hollywood" Henderson and Mike Hegman coming at him fast.

Henderson grabbed Terry's arms and pinned them to the quarterback's sides. Hegman stripped the ball away. He went charging downfield with it. The Steelers gave chase. But they couldn't catch him. Hegman had a 37-yard TD run. And, with the PAT, Dallas had a 14–7 lead.

Bradshaw quickly made up for the play. At his 25, he flipped a short pass to John Stallworth at the 35. Stallworth was being covered by cornerback Aaron Kyle. Kyle threw a tackle as Stallworth caught the ball. But the cornerback missed and went sprawling on the turf. That was all Stallworth needed. He sailed downfield and picked up a couple of blocks. Shifting into high, he outran everyone to the goal line. He had turned a 10-yard pass into a 75-yard scoring play — a new record. Following the PAT, the score was again tied, this time at 14–14.

Pittsburgh broke the deadlock several minutes later. Terry passed for 7 yards to Rocky Bleier in the end zone. It sent the Steelers to the dressing room at halftime with a 21–14 lead.

The Cowboys looked ready to tie things up again early in the third quarter. They worked their way to the Pittsburgh 10. But then came a moment of heartbreaking disappointment.

The trouble came on a third down and three. Coach Tom Landry sent in an extra tight end. He wanted to make it look as if a run was in the works. But Dallas planned to go with a pass. Staubach faded back. He picked out tight end Jackie Smith. Smith pounded into the end zone. Roger threw over the middle to him.

Smith was a fine veteran player. He had gotten himself into the clear. But he slipped on the wet turf. Down he went on his knees. The ball came whistling at him. The throw was low and just slightly to his rear. Jackie managed to get his hands on the ball. Then he dropped it. A sure touchdown was lost.

*Steeler Rocky Bleier takes a short
and sizzling pass. He hit the ground,
but held onto the ball and scored
Pittsburgh's third TD of the day.*

Dallas settled for 3 points on a Rafael Septien field goal.

The score held at 21–17 until the fourth quarter. Then came a controversial play. Working at his own 44, Bradshaw passed as Lynn Swann went racing down the sideline deep into Dallas territory. Running with Swann was his covering man, cornerback Benny Barnes. Barnes was a step or two in front of Lynn as they streaked along.

Terry unloaded a high, arcing bomb. Swann and Barnes glanced back to see it come dropping in. The crowd got ready for one of Lynn's great leaping receptions. But, suddenly, Barnes fell. Perhaps he slipped on the wet turf or was pushed. He went down flat on his face. Swann tripped over him.

As he fell, Lynn grabbed wildly at the ball. But it was beyond his fingertips. It hit the ground at the Dallas 23.

And so did the field judge's yellow flag. Then the field judge was pointing at Barnes for pass interference. He said that Benny had tripped Swann. It had been an accident. But it was still interference.

Benny was furious. He claimed that Swann had pushed him and should be called for offensive interference. The field judge replied that he had seen a bump along the way. But he said that it had taken place far upfield. There had been no push by

Swann at the last second. The call caused an argument among fans that lasted for weeks.

The Steelers now had the ball on the Cowboys' 23. Dallas let them gain just a yard on the next three plays. On third down 9 to go, Pittsburgh tried a trap. It worked perfectly. Franco Harris bulled up the middle for 22 yards and the TD. The score went to 28–17 after the PAT.

The next tally came just 19 seconds later. Helping it along was the wet turf. Roy Gerela slipped as he kicked off. The ball went skipping to defensive tackle Randy White on the Dallas 24. Randy was wearing a cast on a broken left thumb. It caused him to fumble. Somehow, he recovered. Then, as tacklers swarmed in on him, he tried a lateral. The ball never reached his teammate. He saw it roll along the ground. Pittsburgh's Dennis Winston pounced on it at the 18.

Terry Bradshaw wasted no time. He fired an end zone pass to Lynn Swann. Lynn did his usual high flying act. And, as usual, he came down with the ball. In trotted Gerela for the PAT. The score was 35–17.

Pittsburgh's lead now seemed impossible to overcome. But Roger Staubach wasn't finished yet. He engineered a drive from his own 11 to the Steeler 7. A highlight of the march was a 29-yard dash by Tony Dorsett. Roger capped everything off with a TD shot to tight end Billy Joe Dupree. With the PAT, the score looked a little better for Dallas: 35–24.

But the game was grinding down to its final minutes. The Cowboys needed a fast 11 points. Their only chance was an onside kick. It clicked. Dallas took over near midfield.

With blinding speed, the Cowboys hammered their way to the Steeler 4. From there, Staubach stepped back. He sent the ball over the goal line. It landed in the arms of wide receiver Butch Johnson!

The crowd couldn't believe what it was seeing. The Cowboys closed the score to 35–31 with the PAT. Could they get just one more TD? Could they pull off the biggest comeback ever seen in the Super Bowl? There were only 22 seconds left to the final gun.

Another onside kick was in order. The crowd was on its feet. Rafael Septien came to the tee and swung his leg. The Dallas fans groaned. The kick didn't look good. They watched the ball go skipping across midfield. It went to the Pittsburgh 45. Rocky Bleier was waiting there. He threw himself on the ball and pulled it hard against his chest.

Everyone knew the game was over. The Steeler fans went wild. Black-shirted players on the sideline hugged each other. The Dallas fans shook their heads. Their team had come as close to a miracle comeback as you could get. But, even in defeat, the Cowboys had set a record. They had now been in more Super Bowls than any other team — five in all. Their win-loss record stood at 2–3.

Terry Bradshaw fell on the ball for two plays and ran the clock out. The final gun echoed in the damp air. The best of all Super Bowls was now history.

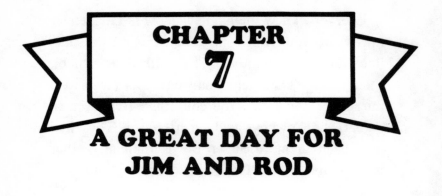

CHAPTER 7

A GREAT DAY FOR JIM AND ROD

The 1970s gave football fans one great moment after another in the Super Bowl. The 1980s would do the same. They opened with a game that set two records.

SUPER BOWL XIV
PITTSBURGH STEELERS (AFC)
vs.
LOS ANGELES RAMS (NFC)

The fans set the first of those two records. There were 103,985 spectators in the Pasadena Rose Bowl stands.

The huge crowd saw Terry Bradshaw throw another of his great passes on that January 20, 1980. The Steelers were trailing 19–17 in the final period. On third down and 8, Terry dropped back. John Stallworth faked a hook and then raced downfield. The ball came sailing in on target. Rams' cornerback Rod Perry jumped to knock it down. But it was just above his fingertips. Stallworth made an over-the-shoulder catch. He was gone for the TD.

The play was good for 73 yards! It left the spectators wide-eyed. And it put the Steelers into the lead. They went on to win 31–19.

The victory set the day's second record. The Steelers had now played in four championship games. They had won them all. They were the "winningest" team in Super Bowl history.

SUPER BOWL XV
OAKLAND RAIDERS (AFC)
vs.
PHILADELPHIA EAGLES (NFC)

This was the first Super Bowl for Coach Dick Vermeil's Eagles. For the Raiders, it was the third. They had played in Super Bowl II under Coach John Rauch. In Super Bowl XI they had played under John Madden. Now Tom Flores was at the helm. More than 75,500 fans made their way into the New Orleans Superdome on January 25, 1981.

The Eagles were slight favorites today. They had knocked the Raiders off 10–7 in a regular season game. Along the way, they had sacked quarterback Jim Plunkett eight times. The Eagles then went on to take the NFC title by walloping Dallas 20–7 in the playoffs.

But the Eagles were in for a disappointing time, for three reasons. First, the Raiders were sore at themselves for letting Philadelphia sack Plunkett so many times. They promised to give him plenty of protection on Super Bowl Sunday. It was a promise they kept. Plunkett was to be sacked just once in the entire game.

The second reason was Jim himself. Plunkett had starred for the New England Patriots (formerly the Boston Patriots) in the early 1970s. Then there had been several poor years with the San Francisco 49ers. Next, Jim came to the Raiders in 1980 as a backup quarterback. He seemed near the end of his playing days. Many fans felt that he was washed up.

But Jim hadn't acted like a washed-up player. He quickly took command when number-one quarterback Dan Pastorini was injured early in the season. He led the Raiders to the wild-card spot in the playoffs. They captured the AFC title by beating the San Diego Chargers 34–27. Oakland became the first wild-card team in the AFC to go all the way. Jim would have fine protection from his teammates in Super Bowl XV. He was going to play one of his best games ever.

Linebacker Rod Martin was to be the third reason for the Eagles' bad day. Rod had started his pro career with Oakland in 1977. But the Raiders had soon traded him away because they were rich in linebackers. They also thought him to be a little too small for the job. Rod stood 6 feet 2 inches (1.8 m) and weighed 215 pounds (97 kg). He was sent to the 49ers.

Then San Francisco dropped him. The Raiders, hit with linebacker injuries, brought him back. In the next years, they watched this "small" man become a star. Rod led all the Oakland linebackers in tackles during the 1980 season. In Super Bowl XV, he was to drive Philadelphia crazy with his interceptions.

He started sending the Eagles up the wall in the first quarter. Philadelphia took the opening kickoff and moved a few yards upfield on two plays. On the next snap, quarterback Ron Jaworski tried a pass. He targeted in on Rod's man, tight end John Spagnola. Both Rod and Spagnola went for the

*Oakland quarterback Jim Plunkett releases
a short pass as Philadelphia's
Ken Clarke (71) and Randy Logan (41)
put the pressure on him.*

ball at the Eagles' 47. But Rod got there first. He tucked the ball away and pounded out 17 yards before being brought down. Rod was on his way to setting a Super Bowl record for interceptions.

The steal gave Jim Plunkett his first chance to shine. In a series of seven plays, he moved to the Philadelphia 2. Along the way, though, the Eagles almost kept Oakland from making a first down. But Jim used a trick cadence as he called signals on a third down play. It pulled the Eagles off-sides. The penalty gave him the yards he needed to keep the drive going.

Once he got to the 2, Jim split his wide receivers — Bob Chandler and Cliff Branch — for a pass. He moved into the pocket. He saw Chandler head into the end zone and pull some of the defense with him. Then Branch was swinging across the goal line. He was in front of his covering man. Jim drilled the ball to Branch. Oakland had its first TD. The score was 7–0 after the PAT.

Oakland had looked good on the drive. On a later series, the Eagles looked just as good. Ron Jaworski connected with receiver Rodney Parker for a 40-yard TD pass. The Philadelphia fans let loose a wild cheer. It turned into a groan. The ball was called back and the score taken away. Wide receiver Harold Carmichael had been in illegal motion on the play.

At that moment, perhaps the Eagles sensed that the day was going to be a disaster. A few minutes later, they *knew* it. The Raiders came up with a play that gave them a record-breaking TD.

Oakland was on its own 20. Plunkett had called for a pass. His primary receiver was to be Bob Chandler. Bob ran his pattern across the middle. But Jim saw that he was strongly covered. Plunkett started looking for a secondary receiver.

The Eagles came charging at the quarterback. They drove him out of the pocket. Jim scrambled wildly. He scooted away from one tackle. All the while, he kept searching for a receiver. Then he sighted Kenny King 19 yards away, up at the 39. King, just behind cornerback Herm Edwards, was waving frantically for the ball.

Jim made his decision. His arm came up and shot forward. He floated an arcing pass to Kenny. The ball just missed Herm Edwards' outstretched hands. It plopped against Kenny's chest. He turned and found a clear field ahead. He and the Eagles then ran a footrace to the goal line. Kenny won.

The play netted 80 yards! It was the longest scoring play in Super Bowl history. Terry Bradshaw's 73-yard toss in Super Bowl XIV was the second longest.

Oakland moved to a 14–0 lead on the PAT. The quarter ended. The stunned Eagles looked at each other. They knew that Plunkett had put in a great 15 minutes of play. He'd thrown four passes. He'd connected every time. Two of the shots had been for touchdowns. The "washed-up" quarterback looked pretty unbeatable.

The game tightened in the second period. Bruising play kept the teams from driving far. Philadelphia, though, managed a field goal. And Plunkett ran into some shaky moments. Again, he tried four passes. But this time, only one was completed. The score stood at 14–3 at halftime.

The Raiders came out looking sharp in the third quarter. They took the opening kickoff and moved 76 yards on five plays. The drive ended when Plunkett fired a 29-yard bullet to Cliff Branch at the goal line. Cliff was being solidly covered by rookie cornerback Roynell Young. Side by side, the two men leaped for the ball. But it was Cliff who pulled it in for keeps. He dropped to the ground and tumbled into the end zone. With the PAT, the score reached 21–3.

The Raiders had been worried about Jim's passing in the second quarter. Now they relaxed a little. He'd gone to the air three times during the 76-yard march. The three passes had picked up 74 of those 76 yards. Jim had his eye back.

But now it was Rod Martin's turn to star again. His moment came midway through the quarter. Philadelphia had a drive going. The Eagles were pushing their way across the midfield stripe. Ron Jaworski tried a shot to the Raider 30. As in the first quarter, his intended receiver was Rod's man, John Spagnola. The crowd held its breath. John seemed to be in the clear as the pass was released.

But Rod closed in on the tight end from the rear. He cut in front of him just as the ball arrived. The "small" linebacker had his second interception of the day — and a 2-yard runback before stepping out of bounds.

The interception seemed to stun the Eagles. They had been on their way to a score. Now, thanks to Rod, they were to fall another 3 points behind. Oakland moved across midfield and went no further. They called on Chris Bahr for a field goal. Chris split the uprights 46 yards away. Oakland's lead went to 24–3.

Still, the Eagles didn't give up completely. Early in the fourth quarter, Jaworski led them to a TD.

That tightened the score a little — to 24–10. But the Raiders came back with a Chris Bahr field goal that moved things to 27–10. The Raiders were just too tough today. The most dejected man on the field had to be Jaworski. By game's end, the "Polish Rifle" would throw 38 passes. He would complete 18 of them for 291 yards. That was more yardage than Plunkett would record. Yet his Eagles were going to lose — thanks to Rod Martin's interceptions.

And there was more to come for Rod. There were just moments left to play. The Eagles were desperately trying for another score. Jaworski passed. He was up against Oakland's prevent defense. The ball sailed into traffic. It went right to Martin.

That did it! Rod Martin had his third interception. It was a Super Bowl record. The linebacker threaded his way for 25 yards. He was grounded at the Philadelphia 38. His teammates crowded around him. They slapped his back and pounded his helmet.

As Rod headed for the bench, he glanced up at the grandstands. Members of his family were seated there, among them his sister Caroline. Caroline had brought him some interesting news just before

Oakland linebacker Rod Martin snags
his third interception in Super Bowl XV.
His three steals set a Super Bowl
record for interceptions.

the game. Two friends, she said, had told her they had a strong feeling that Rod was going to make a Super Bowl interception. How right they had been!

Rod's third interception put an end to the game. Philadelphia's last chance to tighten things was gone. The two teams ground out the final seconds. Super Bowl XV ended with the score 27–10.

The Raiders now had two Super Bowl victories to their credit. Both had been good wins. Both had been by solid margins. But today's victory was extra special. It meant so much to two men.

One was a quarterback who was supposed to be washed up. Jim Plunkett had shown that his career certainly wasn't over. With his team giving him good protection, he'd passed with confidence. He'd thrown 21 times and had hit his target 13 of those times. The passes had netted the Raiders 261 yards. It was a performance that won him the game's MVP award.

The other man was a linebacker once thought too small to play his position. Rod Martin had never believed it. He had become one of the finest defensive players in pro ball. He now held a Super Bowl record that proved just how good he was.

By the time the final gun sounded on January 25, 1981, 13 of the National Football League's 28 teams had played in the Super Bowl. Some had been big winners. Pittsburgh was the biggest. Some had been big losers. But no one can ever really call a team good enough for a championship game a loser. Some had set records. Some had made mistakes and produced crazy plays. But all of them had given millions of fans great moments of football action.

And what of the future? When Super Bowl Sunday rolls around each January, there will be more great moments. You can count on it.

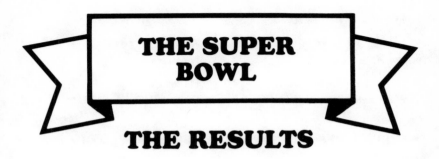

THE SUPER BOWL

THE RESULTS

SUPER BOWL I

January 15, 1967
Los Angeles

Green Bay Packers (NFL)	35
Kansas City Chiefs (AFL)	10

SUPER BOWL II

January 14, 1968
Miami

Green Bay Packers (NFL)	33
Oakland Raiders (AFL)	14

SUPER BOWL III

January 12, 1969
Miami

New York Jets (AFL)	16
Baltimore Colts (NFL)	7

SUPER BOWL IV

January 11, 1970
New Orleans

Kansas City Chiefs (AFL)	23
Minnesota Vikings (NFL)	7

SUPER BOWL V

January 17, 1971
Miami

Baltimore Colts (AFC)	16
Dallas Cowboys (NFC)	13

SUPER BOWL VI

January 16, 1972
New Orleans

Dallas Cowboys (NFC)	24
Miami Dolphins (AFC)	3

SUPER BOWL VII

January 14, 1973
Los Angeles

Miami Dolphins (AFC)	14
Washington Redskins (NFC)	7

SUPER BOWL VIII

January 13, 1974
Houston

Miami Dolphins (AFC)	24
Minnesota Vikings (NFC)	7

SUPER BOWL IX

January 12, 1975
New Orleans

Pittsburgh Steelers (AFC)	16
Minnesota Vikings (NFC)	6

SUPER BOWL X

January 18, 1976
Miami

Pittsburgh Steelers (AFC)	21
Dallas Cowboys (NFC)	17

SUPER BOWL XI

January 9, 1977
Pasadena

Oakland Raiders (AFC)	32
Minnesota Vikings (NFC)	14

SUPER BOWL XII

January 15, 1978
New Orleans

Dallas Cowboys (NFC)	27
Denver Broncos (AFC)	10

SUPER BOWL XIII

January 21, 1979
Miami

Pittsburgh Steelers (AFC)	35
Dallas Cowboys (NFC)	31

SUPER BOWL XIV

January 20, 1980
Pasadena

Pittsburgh Steelers (AFC)	31
Los Angeles Rams (NFC)	19

SUPER BOWL XV

January 25, 1981
New Orleans

Oakland Raiders (AFC)	27
Philadelphia Eagles (NFC)	10

SUPER BOWL XVI

January 24, 1982
Detroit

San Francisco 49ers (NFC)	26
Cincinnati Bengals (AFC)	21

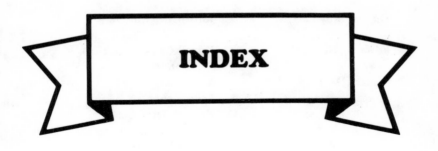

INDEX